By Donna Latham

A Winter Bed

Target Skill Sequence

PEARSON

Scott
Foresman

The chipmunk is looking for a bed for the winter.

Can he sleep in a den?
No, not in a den!

Can he sleep in a pond?
No, not in a pond!

Can he sleep in a nest?
No, not in a nest!

Can he sleep in the leaves?
No, the leaves are not
a good bed for the winter.

Can he sleep in an old tree?
Is an old tree a good bed?

Yes, an old tree is the spot
for a winter nap.

It is a good winter bed.